Be Ye Inspired!

Volume 1

Dr. Cassundra White-Elliott

www.clfpublishing.org
909.315.3161

Cover design by Senir Design. Contact info: info@senirdesign.com

ISBN #978-1-945102-75-2

Printed in the United States of America.

Dedication

To all women, everywhere.

Acknowledgements

I acknowledge every trial, every circumstance, every person, every temptation, and every situation I encountered that led me to my knees, crying out to my Heavenly Father. In life, I have shed many tears as I sought the Lord's guidance. God is faithful and just. Each learning experience was an opportunity to add another ounce of substance to the woman I am today. Oh, bless His name!

Introduction

The purpose of ***Be Ye Inspired!*** is to provide an opportunity for a daily encounter with God. There are exactly 30 days of scripture and exhortation, one to be read each day of an average month. Make a point to read one per day, then reflect on it. Allow the Holy Spirit to minister to you. You might even want to engage one of your friends in a daily discussion about the day's reading.

Cover image - The cover image was chosen due to the exuberant colors it contains and the beautiful butterfly that does its part within nature by pollinating plants. Each woman is a beautiful butterfly, who began as a caterpillar and went through her own unique process of metamorphosis to get to the point in her life where she is today. As a butterfly, you do not have much time to live. So, make the most of each day, and make your life count.

Day One

*"For thou hast possessed my reins: thou hast covered me in my mother's womb. I will praise thee; for **I am fearfully and wonderfully made**: marvellous are thy works; and that my soul knoweth right well. My substance was not hid from thee, when I was made in secret, and curiously wrought in the lowest parts of the earth. Thine eyes did see my substance, yet being unperfect; and in thy book all my members were written, which in continuance were fashioned, when as yet there was none of them."*
Psalm 139:13-16 (KJV)

*"For you created my inmost being; you knit me together in my mother's womb. I praise you because **I am fearfully and wonderfully made**; your works are wonderful, I know that full well. My frame was not hidden from you when I was made in the secret place, when I was woven together in the depths of the earth. Your eyes saw my unformed body; all the days ordained for me were written in your book before one of them came to be."*
Psalm 139:13-16 (NIV)

You were created in the image of Almighty God, the one who knew you from afar off. You are precious in His sight. The works of the Lord are wonderful, which means you are wonderful, as you are God's creation. You must believe you are who God created you to be, even before your physical body came into manifestation. He designed you with purpose, and it is your responsibility to fulfill your purpose in the earth realm. Do not allow your days to pass by aimlessly. Stand up and be counted, as a servant of the Lord, doing what He designed you to do. Regardless of what people may say about your gifts and talents, God placed value and worth within you before you took your first breath. It is up to you to consult with the Lord, so He can show you the assignment He has for you. However, in order to complete your assignment, you must believe that you are fearfully and wonderfully made.

When you are faced with trials, challenges, and adversity, remember who you are. When people walk away and leave you, remember who you are. When the odds are stacked against you, remember who you are. When your friends seem far away and do not understand your journey, remember who you are. You are God's creation! And, you are fearfully and wonderfully made!

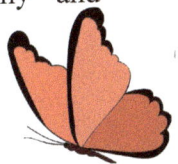

Day Two

"She riseth also while it is yet night, and giveth meat to her household, and a portion to her maidens."
Proverbs 31:15 (KJV)

"She gets up before dawn to prepare breakfast for her household and plan the day's work for her servant girls."
Proverbs 31:15 (NLT)

Time is a great commodity that is given to us by the Lord. And, we are all gifted the same amount of time. We are all given the same amount of minutes in an hour, hours in a day, days in a week, weeks in a month, and months in a year. The difference is how each of us will use the time that has been afforded us.

Make the most of your time. Count it as valuable. Do not squander your time away by procrastinating. As the saying goes, "Why put off for tomorrow what can be done today?"

The virtuous woman in this proverb was a wise woman. She rose up early, while everyone else was yet asleep. She planned not only her day, but she planned the chores of her servants as well. She did not wait for

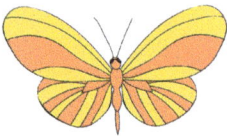

them to come and ask what their chores were. No, she was already ready with a plan.

If she had waited until she was approached, she would have had to come up with something at the spur of the moment. Instead, she had ample time to assess what was necessary and what could wait until the next day or two. Not only that, but she was able to prepare a meal for their consumption, so they would be ready for their day with the energy and strength to carry out their assignments. She was without excuse because she held her time as valuable.

Do you value your time? Do you complete all you can in a given day or do you find excuse after excuse for not completing the required tasks?

Be not slothful. Be about your Father's business. Make each day, each hour, and each minute count.

Day Three

*"**But by the grace of God I am what I am: and his grace which was bestowed upon me was not in vain**; but I laboured more abundantly than they all: yet not I, but the grace of God which was with me."*
I Corinthians 15:10 (KJV)

*"**But by the grace of God I am what I am, and his grace to me was not without effect.** No, I worked harder than all of them—yet not I, but the grace of God that was with me."*
I Corinthians 15:10 (NIV)

The Lord has afforded us all a measure of grace. Like Apostle Paul, do not allow the goodness and the favor of the Lord to be of null effect. Operate in His grace and serve Him, laboring with the love of Christ, understanding that it is not your own power that you work in, but the power of God. When God shows us His favor, it is incumbent upon us to operate in His will, doing that which brings honor unto His name. For, it is by God's grace that we are what and who we are.

Remember, take no credit for yourself for your accomplishments. Without God, you would be nothing and you would have nothing. In all we do, we give all

honor and glory to God.

When people congratulate us on our accomplishments, we should turn their attention to God, so He receives the glory. For, He is the great I Am, and it is in Him that we move, live, and have our being.

We operate to give joy unto the Lord, He is Wonderful, our Counselor, our Way Maker, and our Strong Tower. All we are and all we have is because of His providence.

Day Four

"Nevertheless neither is the man without the woman, neither the woman without the man, in the Lord. For as the woman is of the man, even so is the man also by the woman; but all things of God."
I Corinthians 11:11-12 (KJV)

"Nevertheless, in the Lord woman is not independent of man, nor is man independent of woman. For as woman came from man, so also man is born of woman. But everything comes from God."
I Corinthians 11:11-12 (NIV)

In our society, both men and women are constantly competing against one another, and they like to take credit for all they can. Each sex attempts to outdo the other. Despite our best efforts to supersede one another, we are reminded by the above verse that neither man nor woman is independent of one another. Rather, we must depend upon each other to get our tasks done, remembering that everything comes from God.

As the creator, God was cognizant of our interconnectedness before He created us. He designed us in a manner that would not allow us to exist void of the other without some degree of discomfort.

When we attempt to operate without the opposite sex, we find ourselves lagging and incomplete. So, rather than pretend the opposite sex is unneeded, find ways to co-exist and appreciate the abilities of every person. We should strive to pull out the best in one another rather than downplay a person's strengths. Doing so will enable us to go further and accomplish more for the kingdom.

Day Five

"Whose adorning let it not be that outward adorning *of plaiting the hair, and of wearing of gold, or of putting on of apparel; But* **let it be** *the hidden man of the heart, in that which is not corruptible,* **even the ornament** *of a meek and quiet spirit, which is in the sight of God of great price."*
I Peter 3:3-4 (KJV)

"Your beauty should not come from outward adornment, such as elaborate hairstyles and the wearing of gold jewelry or fine clothes. Rather, **it should be that of your inner self, the unfading beauty of a gentle and quiet spirit,** *which is of great worth in God's sight."*
I Peter 3:3-4 (NIV)

Oftentimes, we are more concerned about our outward appearance rather than the condition of our inner man. Too much stock is placed in what we choose to adorn ourselves (clothing, jewelry, hairstyles, and make-up) with instead of the countenance we house within us. Galatians 5:22-23 tell us about the nine fruit of the spirit: love, joy, peace, longsuffering, gentleness, goodness, faith, meekness, and temperance.

What difference would it make if we take excessive amounts of time to ensure that our outer appearance is stellar, but internally, we wreak of sewage, spewing out venom of hatred, animosity, greed, bitterness, discontentment, vile words, anger, unforgiveness, envy, jealousy, and malice?

When it comes to making positive changes in our personal life, we should begin by taking inventory of our emotional and mental state. When we are emotionally and mentally unhealthy, we will find it difficult to operate in the fruits of the spirit. If we find within ourselves unhealthy emotions and having unhealthy thoughts, which leads to unhealthy actions (sin), we need to go before God for a cleansing. Once we work on our inner man and are in a healthy condition spiritually, then we can work on the outside.

Day Six

"*She considereth a field, and buyeth it*: with the fruit
of her hands she planteth a vineyard."
Proverbs 31:16 (KJV)

"*She considers a field before she buys or accepts it*
[expanding her business prudently]; With her profits
she plants fruitful vines in her vineyard."
Proverbs 31:16 (AB)

A prudent business woman considers all aspects of starting and running a business prior to making the final decision to enter into the endeavor. She weighs the pros and cons. She operates with the leading of the Holy Spirit who will tell her what type of business she should embark upon and when the time is right to make the investment. Then, after she launches her business, she works diligently to make it profitable. She is not only wise, but she is prudent as well. Being prudent keeps her from being overzealous and constrains her in the boundaries of wisdom.

Remember though, we do not rely upon our own strength and wisdom to operate our business. We must remember at all times, it is God who gives us the power to gain wealth and not we ourselves.

Running a business is not always an easy thing to do, and quite frankly, we will not always know which choice is the right choice because both or several options may be viable. Therefore, it is incumbent upon us to seek the Lord for guidance and wisdom. James 1:5 says, *"If any of you lack wisdom, let him ask of God, that giveth to all men liberally, and upbraideth not; and it shall be given him."* God is not only our source, but He is a resource, and we can go to Him at any time. Reach out to Him today!

Day Seven

"*I will bless the LORD at all times: his praise shall continually be in my mouth. My soul shall make her boast in the LORD: the humble shall hear thereof, and be glad. O magnify the LORD with me, and let us exalt his name together. I sought the LORD, and he heard me, and delivered me from all my fears.*"
Psalm 34:1-4 (KJV)

"*I will extol the LORD at all times; his praise will always be on my lips. I will glory in the LORD; let the afflicted hear and rejoice. Glorify the LORD with me; let us exalt his name together. I sought the LORD, and he answered me; he delivered me from all my fears.*"
Psalm 34:1-4 (NIV)

The Lord has truly been good to us our entire lives through. Even in the midst of challenges, even when we had to go without, even when we felt like "when it rain, it pours." God has truly been good, and for that, I will praise Him all the days of my life. I will tell of His goodness. I will tell of His tender mercies. I will exalt His holy name. I will always have a praise on my lips.

Heavenly Father,

You have always been good to me. You have loved me when I was unlovable. You have sheltered me in the midst of a storm. You have protected me when harm circled about me. You kept my children and grand-children safe. You stretched dollars to meet the needs. You showed me kindness when I was unkind. You showed me favor when I was selfish. You made a way when I could not see my way clear. You made every crooked path straight. Lord, you healed me when I was sick. Lord, even more than all of that, you paid the price for the penalty of my sins, for my transgressions, for my iniquities. Lord, I owe you my life, and I surrender it unto you. Thank you for dumping my sin into the sea of forgetfulness.

Lord, thank you for imputing your righteousness unto me. Thank you for washing me white as snow. Thank you for allowing me the honor to approach your throne of grace. Lord, thank you for all you have ever done, all that you continue to do, and all that you will do in the future.

In the name of Jesus,

Amen.

Day Eight

"Both riches and honour come of thee, and thou reignest over all; and in thine hand is power and might; and in thine hand it is to make great, and to give strength unto all."

I Chronicles 29:12 (KJV)

"Wealth and honor come from you alone, for you rule over everything. Power and might are in your hand, and at your discretion people are made great and given strength."

I Chronicles 29:12 (NLT)

Many people spend most of their adulthood striving for power, fame, and riches. Sometimes, it is at the expense of friendships, coworkers, and loved ones. Matthew 6:33 advises, *"But seek first the kingdom of God and His righteousness, and all these things shall be added to you."* If we seek a relationship with the Heavenly Father, He will give us the desires of our heart (Psalm 37:4). It is in Him that we live, move, and have our being (Acts 17:28). And, He is the one who brings about elevation in the lives of the believers. And, it is done at His discretion.

Then, when He gives us positions, authority, and power, He will give us the strength to endure the challenges that come along with newly acquired responsibility and great wealth.

Let us pray.

Heavenly Father,

I look to you in all I do and for all I hope to be. I understand it is at your discretion whether or not I am promoted, elevated, gain wealth, or prosper. Lord God, I thank you for every transition in my life that leads me to where you desire me to be. I thank you for divine favor, protection, and the journey. Bless me oh Lord and order my steps. Make every crooked path straight and give me your wisdom. I thank you Lord, and I bless your name.

Day Nine

*"Wait on the LORD: be of good courage, and he shall
strengthen thine heart: wait, I say, on the LORD."*
Psalm 27:14 (KJV)

*"Wait patiently for the LORD. Be brave and
courageous. Yes, wait patiently for the LORD."*
Psalm 27:14 (NLT)

"Wait!" is typically not something we like to be told
by other people. Additionally, telling ourselves to *wait*
is equally and sometimes even harder to do. But when
we are effectively operating in the spirit, we must learn
to exercise patience. Remember, God does not operate
within our timeframe. He is a great judge, and He is all-
knowing and wise. He knows the best time for events to
occur in our life.

Trusting in the Lord means trusting completely in
His wisdom and in His timing. This verse tells us to
wait and while doing so, we are to be of good courage.
We are not to wait grudgingly or to murmur (complain)
while doing so. Instead, we are to hold onto the belief
that God will bring about the best outcome for us.
Being of good courage means to be of good cheer,

having the joy and happiness of knowing that at the end of our season of waiting, God will have performed a far better result than we could have if we had operated in our own strength and with our limited wisdom.

Day Ten

"In God I will praise his word, in God I have put my trust; I will not fear what flesh can do unto me."
Psalm 56:4 (KJV)

"In God, whose word I praise - in God I trust and am not afraid. What can mere mortals do to me?"
Psalm 56:4 (NIV)

Mankind can be very cruel to one another, from giving evil looks, doing misdeeds, slandering someone's name to engaging in homicide, rape, manslaughter, robberies, to promoting racism, marginalizing others, causing economic disparities, and breeding inequities. If there is a specific manner of evil, mankind has engaged in it.

Regardless of the physical, emotional, financial, psychological, and sexual harm mankind can inflict upon one another, mankind is limited when it comes to impacting one's spirit. One's spirit can be wounded or broken, but it cannot be desecrated or destroyed as the body can. So, rather than concern ourselves about what mortals can do to our physical body, we need to ensure that our spirit is aligned with the Holy Spirit, allowing

Him to guide our paths throughout our lifetime. If our spirit is in tune with God's spirit, we will be sustained. If one's spirit man is strong, a person can be sustained.

Heavenly Father,

I come before your throne of grace, giving you praise, honor, and glory. Lord, I pray you will give me sustenance for my spirit, so that I may be strong in you. Your Word tells me to keep my head uplifted towards the hills, for my help comes from you. Lord, I depend on you for my livelihood and my spiritual strength. My faith is strong, and I will continue to stand on your Word. I submit this prayer in the name of my Lord and Savior Jesus Christ.

Amen.

Day Eleven

"Cause me to hear thy lovingkindness in the morning; for in thee do I trust: cause me to know the way wherein I should walk; for I lift up my soul unto thee."
Psalm 143:8 (KJV)

"Let the morning bring me word of your unfailing love, for I have put my trust in you. Show me the way I should go, for to you I entrust my life."
Psalm 143:8 (NIV)

Life is filled with decisions to be made. Some decisions will be easy to make, while others will be a bit more challenging due to the different options that are presented to us. To make decisions, we use information we are provided and/or our experiences. Quite frankly, it is difficult to know whether we are making the correct decision for ourselves because we do not know the end result of our choices. Therefore, to prevent running into one roadblock after another or finding ourselves at a fork in the road and not knowing whether to go to the left or to the right, we should consult our Heavenly Father for guidance.

In the book of Psalms, we are told in Division 37, Verse 23 that the steps of a good man are ordered by the Lord. A woman who fully trusts in God allows the Lord to lead and guide her through the pathways of life. In the book of Jeremiah, we are told that God knows our ending from our beginning. He is the one who created us, and He knows His purpose for designing us. Therefore, He knows which path we should take to walk into our pre-orchestrated destiny.

Day Twelve

"Now unto him that is able to do exceeding abundantly above all that we ask or think, according to the power that worketh in us, Unto him be glory in the church by Christ Jesus throughout all ages, world without end. Amen."
Ephesians 3:20-21 (KJV)

"Now to him who is able to do immeasurably more than all we ask or imagine, according to his power that is at work within us, to him be glory in the church and in Christ Jesus throughout all generations, for ever and ever! Amen."
Ephesians 3:20-21 (NIV)

God can do so much more for us than what our limited minds can think or even dream. And, He does it by His power that is working within us. If we yield ourselves as willing vessels for the Lord's use, He can effectuate His will for our lives. But first, we must believe that He exists (Hebrews 11:6); second, we must believe He will withhold no good thing from us (Psalm 84:11); and we must believe He wants the best for us (3 John 1:2).

God is our all in all. He is our source. He is our Way Maker. He is the great I Am. He is the Alpha and the Omega. He is the potter, and we are the clay. He is Jehovah Rapha. He is Jehovah Jireh. He is Jehovah Tsidkenu. He is our Wonderful Counselor. He is our lawyer in the courtroom. He is a doctor in the sick room. He **is** all we need Him to be!

Day Thirteen

"Strength and honour are *her clothing; and she shall rejoice in time to come. She openeth her mouth with wisdom; and in her tongue is the law of kindness."*
Proverbs 31:25-26 (KJV)

"She is clothed with strength and dignity; she can laugh at the days to come. She speaks with wisdom, and faithful instruction is on her tongue."
Proverbs 31:25-26 (NIV)

James Chapter 3 tells us that the tongue is a wicked and unruly member. Proverbs 18 Verse 21 tells us life and death are both in the power of the tongue. As with anything else in life, we have a choice as to how we utilize our tongue. This particular verse tells us to use our tongue to speak with wisdom and to exercise kindness.

Many times, especially when we have been hurt, we have a tendency to spew venom from our tongues in an effort to cut down, hurt, torture, and maim another person. Instead of doing that, we should use our tongue to encourage another person, to lift someone up when

he/she is down, to share the Word of the Lord, to demonstrate our faith, to share a testimony, to put a smile on someone's face, and to demonstrate that all is not lost. The only way to become capable of using our tongue for good rather than for trickery or deceit is to ensure that our heart is cleansed of all unforgiveness and unrighteousness. When our heart is filled with love, patience, kindness, grace and mercy, our words will demonstrate those characteristics.

Day Fourteen

"But the Lord is faithful, who shall stablish you,
and <u>keep you from evil</u>."
II Thessalonians 3:3 (KJV)

"But the Lord is faithful, and He will strengthen and
<u>*protect you from the evil one*</u>*."*
II Thessalonians 3:3 (NASB)

According to Job 1:10, the Lord can place a hedge of protection around you. The function of the hedge is two-fold. First, it will protect you from the wiles of the enemy, our adversary, who roams about as a roaring lion to and fro across the earth seeking whom he can devour (I Peter 5:8). Second, the hedge keeps you safe from evil by providing you with a way of escape (II Corinthians 10:13). That means although you may be tempted by evil, you will not automatically be overtaken by it unless you so choose. God will always provide a method for escape. It's up to you to take it.

Heavenly Father,

Help me to know good from evil and right from wrong. When I am tempted, please help me acknowledge and to take the way of escape you have provided for me. Lord, I thank you for protecting me.

In Jesus' name.

Amen.

Day Fifteen

"But they that wait upon the LORD shall renew *their strength; they shall mount up with wings* as eagles; <u>**they shall run, and not be weary;** and *they shall walk, and not faint*</u>*."*
Isaiah 40:31 (KJV)

"Yet those who wait for the LORD Will gain new strength; They will mount up with *wings like eagles,* <u>***They will run and not get tired,***</u> <u>***They will walk and not become weary***</u>*."*
Isaiah 40:31 (NASB)

The cares of this world can wear us down, even when we attempt to do good, be positive, and follow God's ordinances. Through it all, the Lord will provide us with sustenance, giving us strength for the journey. He will also provide us with His providence, making sure our needs are met.

When we choose to run the race, striving for the prize of the high calling of God in Christ Jesus, we will not grow weary. We will endure to the end. When we find ourselves faced with trials and battles, we will

walk through the fire without fainting. God will be with us every step of the way. In Him, we can put our trust. In Him, we can develop our faith. In Him, there is no failure. In Him, all things are possible.

Lord Father,

I thank you for your divine covering of protection over my life. You have provided me shelter from the storm, protection during perilous times, and from hurt, harm and danger. Lord, I thank you for your grace and tender mercies that are restored to me each and every day. Thank you for loving me and keeping me safe.

In Jesus' name,

Amen.

Day Sixteen

"**Blessed is the man that trusteth in the LORD**, and whose hope the LORD is. For he shall be as a tree planted by the waters, and that spreadeth out her roots by the river, and shall not see when heat cometh, but her leaf shall be green; and shall not be careful in the year of drought, neither shall cease from yielding fruit."
Jeremiah 17:7-8 (KJV)

"**Blessed [with spiritual security] is the man who believes and trusts in and relies on the LORD** And whose hope and confident expectation is the LORD. For he will be [nourished] like a tree planted by the waters, That spreads out its roots by the river; And will not fear the heat when it comes; But its leaves will be green and moist. And it will not be anxious and concerned in a year of drought nor stop bearing fruit."
Jeremiah 17:7-8 (AB)

Exercising one's faith in the Lord results in great benefits, such as having stability. When your faith is strong and you trust God with your life, you will

become firmly planted instead of blowing about with every wind of doctrine (Ephesians 4:14). Then, as a further benefit, you will begin to grow roots that will further stabilize your life as a child of God.

To gain the benefit of stability, you must do the following:

1. Hear the Word of God to strengthen your faith (Romans 10:17).
2. Do the Word. Act on your faith (James 1:22).
3. Share the Word. (II Timothy 4:5).

Day Seventeen

"Beloved, <u>I wish above all things that thou mayest prosper and be in health</u>, even as thy soul prospereth."
III John 1:2 (KJV)

"Dear friend, <u>I pray that you may enjoy good health and that all may go well with you</u>, even as your soul is getting along well."
III John 1:2 (NIV)

Our gracious Lord is always concerned about our needs as well as the desires of our heart. In all things that concern us, He wants us to prosper. Prosperity is usually viewed in connection with financial wealth. However, to limit the scope of prosperity to only finances would be to limit prosperity at its core. We can prosper in a variety of areas, including but not limited to physical health, mental wellness, relationships, job/career, family life, positions of leadership and, of course, financial wealth.

Then, according to this verse, God wants us to be in good health: physically, emotionally, financially, psychologically, relationally, and sexually. That means

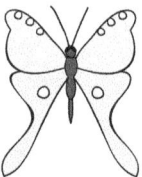

being free of addictions, all manner of abuse, and exorbitant debt.

Jehovah Rapha, my god and my healer,

Thank you for keeping me in perfect health, free from infirmities, free from illness and disease, free from famine and noisome pestilence. Thank you for keeping me healthy, safe, and whole.

In Jesus' name,

Amen.

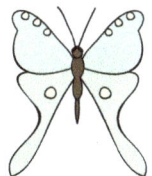

Day Eighteen

"Likewise the Spirit also helpeth our infirmities: for we know not what we should pray for as we ought: <u>but the Spirit itself maketh intercession for us with groanings which cannot be uttered.</u>"
Romans 8:26 (KJV)

"In the same way, the Spirit helps us in our weakness. We do not know what we ought to pray for, <u>but the Spirit himself intercedes for us through wordless groans.</u>"
Romans 8:26 (NIV)

When we approach the Lord's throne of grace when we pray, the Lord desires sincere prayers, rather than those recited by rote memorization. And although prayer comes from our heart, we do not always know for what to pray. In our times of uncertainty, the Holy Spirit comes to our aide, offering indecipherable groans. Thus, we pray in the spirit, allowing the Holy Spirit to have His way, for He is the omniscient, omnipresent, and omnipotent one, and He knows what the needs are. So, He assists us in making our request known to the Father.

Holy Spirit,

You know my heart. You understand my deepest wants and needs, and you know my every intention. You know me better than I know myself. There is nowhere I could run to escape your presence, and nothing I could hide from you!

And that's why, right now, I am asking you to give me your divine wisdom and guidance.

I don't always know what to pray for. My soul is weary, and I am tired. I often worry about making the right decision—but I *want* to live a life that honors you. Even though I may feel like I can't move forward or see what's ahead—you see me. And, you know me. So, please guide me. Show me the paths that lead to abundant life, and convict me when I am tempted to stray from you.

As you guide me, restore me. I will place my hope in you at all times because you know all things, and by you, my life is held together. You are my strength in times of need, and you have become my salvation.

So hold me close, Lord, and teach me to walk in a manner worthy of the calling you have given me. Direct my steps as you guard my life, because I want to glorify you.

In Jesus' name,
Amen.

Day Nineteen

*"I can do all things through Christ which
strengtheneth me."*
Philippians 4:13 (KJV)

*"I can do all things through Christ who
gives me strength."*
Philippians 4:13 (BSB)

There will be times in our life when we are faced with a task that may appear insurmountable and possibly unattainable. We may even be gripped with fear due to the enormity of the task that lies ahead. But God's Word tells us that He has not given us the spirit of fear, but of power, love, and a sound mind (II Timothy 1:7). If we truly trust the Lord and lean not to our own understanding and operate in the power He has afforded us, the task will become manageable. Remember, in Luke 10:19, it is written, *"Behold, I give unto you power to tread on serpents and scorpions, and over all the power of the enemy: and nothing shall by any means hurt you."* We must understand the power and authority we possess as children of the Most High. Then, and only then, will we

be able to forge ahead with the confidence He has given us.

We must believe that we are able to do all things with the Lord's leading. We must believe that we are equipped for the task with which we are presented. We must believe that we are overcomers. We must understand that the Lord is with us at all times, because He told us that He would not forsake us. We must stand tall with our back straight and our mind fixed. Then, while having on the full armor of God, we must press toward the mark, with the determination that we **will** attain the prize of the high calling of God in Christ Jesus (Philippians 3:14).

Day Twenty

"The LORD is my rock, and my fortress, and my deliverer; my God, my strength, in whom I will trust; my buckler, and the horn of my salvation, and my high tower."
Psalm 18:2 (KJV)

"The LORD is my rock, my fortress, and my savior; my God is my rock, in whom I find protection. He is my shield, the power that saves me, and my place of safety."
Psalm 18:2 (NLT)

This verse reminds us that God is our all in all. He is our everything. In Him, there is no lack. In Him, all needs are met. In Him, life is sustainable.

On the next page is a chart that provides the various names for God. Read through them. Call on Him by the appropriate name when you have a specific need.

Knowing the various names of God keeps us in tune with all He provides for us.

1. El Roi- The God Who Sees (Genesis 16:13)

2. El Shaddai- The All-Sufficient God (Genesis 17:1)

3. El Elyon- The Most High God (Psalm 9:2)

4. Adonai- Lord, Master (Psalm 16:2)

5. Jehovah Nissi- The Lord My Banner (Exodus 17:15)

6. Jehovah Raah- The Lord My Shepherd (Psalm 23)

7. Jehovah Rapha- The Lord That Heals (Exodus 15:26)

8. Jehovah Shammah- The Lord Is There (Ezekiel 48:35)

9. Jehovah Tsidkenu- The Lord Our Righteousness (Jeremiah 33:16)

10. Jehovah Mekoddishkem- The Lord Who Sanctifies You (Leviticus 20:8)

11. El Olam- The Everlasting God (Isaiah 26:4)

12. Jehovah Jireh- The Lord Will Provide (Genesis 22:14)

13. Jehovah Shalom- The Lord Is Peace (Judges 6:24)

14. Jehovah Sabaoth- The Lord Of Hosts (Isaiah 5:16)

15. Elohim Ozer Li- God My Helper (Psalm 54:4)

16. El Sali- God My Rock (II Samuel 22:47)

17. El Simchath Gill- God My Exceeding Joy (Psalm 43:4)

18. Jehovah Gibbor Milchamah- The LORD Mighty In Battle (Psalm 24:8)

19. Jehovah El Emeth- LORD God Of Truth (Psalm 31:5)

20. Jehovah Hoshiah- O LORD Save (Psalm 20:9)

21. Sar Shalom- Prince of Peace (Isaiah 9:6)

Day Twenty-One

"Thine, O LORD, is the greatness, and the power, and the glory, and the victory, and the majesty: for all that is in the heaven and in the earth is thine; thine is the kingdom, O LORD, and <u>thou art exalted as head above all</u>."
I Chronicles 29:11 (KJV)

"Yours, LORD, is the greatness and the power and the glory and the splendor and the majesty, for everything in the heavens and on earth belongs to you. Yours, LORD, is the kingdom, and <u>you are exalted as head over all</u>."
I Chronicles 29:11 (CSB)

In Genesis, the book of beginnings, we are informed about how God created the heavens, the earth, and everything that is contained within the earth, including the land, the waters, the animals, the vegetation, and the humans. Genesis 2:7 says God formed man from the dust of the ground. Then, He breathed the breath of life into his nostrils, and man became a living soul. Isaiah 64:8 says, *"But now, O LORD, thou art our father; we are the clay, and thou our potter; and we all are the work of thy hand,"* thus reiterating God is the creator.

As the creator, God is fully in control of the universe and all that it encompasses. We are to exalt His name, giving Him the honor and glory that is due to Him and Him alone. For He is the Almighty God! His name is to be exalted above every other name. He is to be exalted above every person, every creature, and all material things. No one and nothing should receive more praise or attention over the Father.

Day Twenty-Two

"Therefore, my beloved brethren, be ye stedfast, unmoveable, always abounding in the work of the Lord, forasmuch as ye know that your labour is not in vain in the Lord."
I Corinthians 15:58 (KJV)

"Therefore, my dear brothers and sisters, stand firm. Let nothing move you. Always give yourselves fully to the work of the Lord, because you know that your labor in the Lord is not in vain."
I Corinthians 15:58 (NIV)

Even the most faithful of Christians who labor in the vineyard of the Lord sometimes feels as though their service is thankless work and often goes overlooked and unappreciated. That belief, however, is a lie from the enemy. A lie that is spread to discourage faithful servants. Apostle Paul tells us here that we will be rewarded for our earthly service. The reward could be while we're here on earth, or the reward could be later in the afterlife (in heaven), or the reward could be in both places.

The key though is not to serve for the benefit of rewards, but to serve with a servant's heart, one that is fully dedicated to see the work of the kingdom carried out: the saving of lost souls. Our job on earth is to spread the gospel of the Good News of Jesus Christ, which is His death, burial, and resurrection. It is our job to point people toward heaven, to point people toward God. If we do that and make that our singular focus, we will have a great reward in heaven.

Day Twenty-Three

"Oh, how great is Your goodness, Which You have laid up for those who fear You, Which You have prepared for those who trust in You In the presence of the sons of men!"
Psalm 31:19 (KJV)

"How abundant are the good things that you have stored up for those who fear you, that you bestow in the sight of all, on those who take refuge in you."
Psalm 31:19 (NIV)

According to Ephesians 2:8, by grace we are saved through faith. It is our faith that allows us entry into the family of God, making us the adopted sons and daughters of God. As His children, we then become co-heirs with Christ Jesus. It is this relationship that affords us the opportunity to be awarded by our Heavenly Father with good gifts.

The good gifts and favor that we are granted while we are here on earth is not done in secret. God will make His favor toward us known amongst men. Because of our faith, we will be rewarded on earth, while receiving our

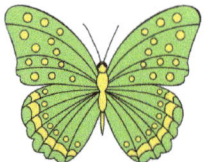

full inheritance in the future, after standing at the Judgment Seat.

What is God's reasoning for awarding our faith while we are here on earth? It is to serve as a testimony to a faithless generation who has yet to exercise faith in a loving god. When unbelievers see the joy and fullness of the life of a believer as a result of their reverence for God the creator, it gives them an opportunity to consider their own life and their own ways.

So, be an example today as a servant of God who has found favor therein.

Day Twenty-Four

"When thou passest through the waters, I will be with thee; and through the rivers, they shall not overflow thee: when thou walkest through the fire, thou shalt not be burned; neither shall the flame kindle upon thee."
Isaiah 43:2 (KJV)

"When you go through deep waters, I will be with you. When you go through rivers of difficulty, you will not drown. When you walk through the fire of oppression, you will not be burned up; the flames will not consume you."
Isaiah 43:2 (NLT)

In Deuteronomy 31:6, we are told that the Lord will not leave or forsake us. In that, we can take comfort, knowing the Lord will always be by our side. In this verse though, we receive added benefits of protection. Not only will the Lord be with us, but He will not allow the rivers to overflow onto us. In fiery trials, He will keep us from being burned and keep all flames from even kindling upon us.

The Lord knows we will face troubling times, trials, and even times of tribulation. However, through it all, we will have His comfort and peace that surpasses all under-

standing.

Let's say a prayer of thanksgiving for the Lord's kindness.

Jehovah Jireh,

I thank you for being a loving and protective god who cares for His children, providing an arc of safety. No matter what I go through and no matter what I may face, you will be there by my side, every step of the way. And for that, I thank you, God. You are my help, my protector, my all-in-all, my Way Maker, my guide, my defender. Lord, I love you, and I bless your holy name.

Amen

Day Twenty-Five

*"Be not wise in thine own eyes: fear the LORD, and
depart from evil. It shall be health to thy navel,
and marrow to thy bones."*
Proverbs 3:7-8 (KJV)

*"Be not wise in your own eyes; fear the LORD, and turn
away from evil. It will be healing to your flesh
and refreshment to your bones."*
Proverbs 3:7-8 (ESV)

As a society of educated beings, we have been taught to think, to research, and to explore in an effort to gain knowledge and to search for answers. At the same time, we have been taught that we can trust experts and their findings. So, we have come to rely on doctors and scientists, etc.

As a believer, we are taught to exercise our faith, to take God at His Word and to do so without doubting. We are to understand that God is all-wise and all-knowing, and even though our brains are designed to think, comprehend, and draw conclusions, we are no match for the wisdom God possesses.

So, to be not wise in our own eyes simply means to not consider ourselves superior or smart or intelligent enough that we do not need to seek God for guidance in all things that concern our lives. If we elect to believe we do not need godly wisdom, we will find ourselves ensnared in far more troubling situations than we would have if we had consulted Him.

Day Twenty-Six

*"The LORD is my shepherd; I shall not want. He maketh
me to lie down in green pastures: he leadeth me beside
the still waters. He restoreth my soul: he leadeth me in the
paths of righteousness for his name's sake. Yea, though I
walk through the valley of the shadow of death, I will fear
no evil: for thou art with me; thy rod and thy staff they
comfort me. Thou preparest a table before me in the
presence of mine enemies: thou anointest my head with
oil; my cup runneth over. Surely goodness and mercy
shall follow me all the days of my life: and I will dwell in
the house of the LORD for ever."*
Psalm 23 (KJV)

Although our life may be filled with trials, snares, disappointments, and unforeseen circumstances, the Lord provides His grace and mercy for us. No matter what we may encounter, He always has peace, calmness, tender mercies, and His protection available for us. In Him, there is no lack. In Him is righteousness. In Him, there is restoration. In Him, there is no fear. In Him, there is comfort. In Him, there is abundance. In Him, there is anointing. In Him, there is plenty. In Him, there is mercy. In Him, there is goodness. In Him, there is shelter. In Him, there is everything we need.

He is our shepherd, and we shall not want. As a shepherd, God shows cares and tender affection toward His flock. He takes us into His fold and cares for us, protects us, and provides for us, with more care, making it His business to keep the flock. As God has taking on the responsibility of being our shepherd, as sheep we must be inoffensive, meek, and quiet, listening and following His instructions. We must know His voice and follow only Him.

In the Lord, our every need is met. In the green pastures of the Lord, food is provided, and the Word of life is nourishment to us. His Word is milk for babes; it is never barren. His Word gives us a place to lie down, giving us quiet contentment for our own minds. Our souls are well at ease in Him, and in Him, we can take our rest.

In Him, we can find restoration. When we wander away from the sheepfold, God is able to show us our error, allow us to repent, and will receive us back again. Without His hand upon our life and His willingness to restore us, we would wander aimlessly about the world, finding ourselves in a lost condition. Also, restoration is supplied as it relates to our health condition. When our body has become fatigued and may be ailing with illness, the Lord can restore us back to proper health.

Finally, the Lord protects us from our enemies, and He even goes as far as to celebrate, uplift, and elevate us in the presence of our enemies, showing His favor upon our lives.

And then there is the Lord's anointing. The Holy Spirit pours Himself onto, anoints, and then empowers believers to perform special tasks from God to accomplish His purposes.

Day Twenty-Seven

*"**If my people, which are called by my name, shall humble themselves, and pray, and seek my face, and turn from their wicked ways**; then will I hear from heaven, and will forgive their sin, and will heal their land."*
II Chronicles 7:14 (KJV)

*"**If my own people will humbly pray and turn back to me and stop sinning**, then I will answer them from heaven. I will forgive them and make their land fertile once again."*
II Chronicles 7:14 (CEV)

As humans, we sometimes have a tendency to seek the hand of God and His favor while living anyway we choose. Our choices may not line up with God's Word, but yet and still, we somehow have the expectation that He will honor us regardless of our behavior and our disobedience. This verse tells us clearly that the Lord has expectations of us, and when we adhere to His expectations, He will withhold no good thing from us.

Our relationship with the Lord is a two-way street. God expects that His people who are called by His name, if they have dishonored His name by their iniquity, should honor it by accepting the punishment of their iniquity.

They must humble themselves under His hand, must pray for the removal of the judgment, must seek the face of God; and yet all this will not do unless they turn from their wicked ways and return to God from whom they have revolted.

God expects us, as His children, to submit ourselves humbly before Him. He expects us to be in constant communication with Him through the vehicle of prayer. He expects us to not walk in the ways of sin, transgressing against Him. When we adhere to the expectations of the Lord, then we can expect Him to answer our pleas and requests in return.

Day Twenty-Eight

"Peace I leave with you, my peace I give unto you: not as the world giveth, give I unto you. Let not your heart be troubled, neither let it be afraid."
John 14:27 (KJV)

"I am leaving you with a gift—peace of mind and heart. And the peace I give is a gift the world cannot give. So don't be troubled or afraid."
John 14:27 (NLT)

According to Matthew Henry's Commentary, when Christ was about to leave the world, He made His will. His soul was committed to His Father in heaven. His body was bequeathed to Joseph, to be decently interred. His clothes fell to the soldiers. His mother was left in the care of John. And, for His disciples, He left His peace. That is peace with God, peace with one another, and peace in our own bosoms meant for a tranquil mind arising from a sense of our justification before God.

The world system gives us a false sense of peace, one that can be easily taken away just as easy as it was provided. In the Lord, however, we can find true peace that will stay with us regardless of difficult situations we

may encounter.

The Bible tells us in Proverbs 4:7, wisdom is the principal thing and that in our getting of wisdom, we must get understanding. So, when we read here in this verse about the Lord's peace and all that comes with it, it is important to take the Lord at His Word when He says His peace is not like the world's peace and because of that, we have no reason to be afraid or to let our heart be troubled. What the Lord is providing us here is a confidence that we can only find in Him knowing that because of the love He has for us, He will protect us on every side and in every situation and in every moment.

Day Twenty-Nine

"Be careful for nothing; but in <u>every thing by prayer and supplication with thanksgiving let your requests be made known unto God</u>. And the peace of God, which passeth all understanding, shall keep your hearts and minds through Christ Jesus."
Philippians 4:6-7 (KJV)

"Do not be anxious about anything, but <u>in every situation, by prayer and petition, with thanksgiving, present your requests to God</u>. And the peace of God, which transcends all understanding, will guard your hearts and your minds in Christ Jesus."
Philippians 4:6-7 (NIV)

In our day-to-day life experiences, we will most certainly have concerns that arise. When we experience those concerns, it would do us well to avoid becoming filled with anxiety. Anxiety can lead to making unwise and untimely choices. Instead, we are directed to approach the Lord in prayer, petitioning Him for guidance and assistance in dealing with the issues at hand. When we consult the all-wise God, we demonstrate to Him where we have placed our trust.

Notice this, we are to not only take the concerning situations to the Lord in prayer, but we are to take all things to Him in prayer. Prayer is an opportunity to ease our mind of anything that is burdensome, causing us to be perplexed and/or distressed. Then, we join thanksgiving with our prayers and supplication. Not only do we seek God for our supplies of good, but we render unto Him receipts of mercy. Thereby, we gratefully acknowledge all of His blessings.

Yes, God is all knowing, but when He hears our request directly from our lips, it shows our dependence upon Him as our savior and protector. Also, there is a further consequence that results from our prayers: we will receive the peace of God, which will transcend all understanding, allowing our hearts and minds to be guarded in Jesus Christ.

Day Thirty

"Wisdom is the principal thing; therefore get wisdom: and with all thy getting get understanding."
Proverbs 4:7 (KJV)

"Getting wisdom is the wisest thing you can do! And whatever else you do, develop good judgment."
Proverbs 4:7 (NLT)

Throughout the years of our lifetime, there are many things we seek after, including job positions and promotions; better, stronger and long-lasting relationships; good health and fit bodies; the best neighborhood to raise our families; the most affordable and beneficial vacation locations, and the list goes on.

Proverbs 4:7 informs us that wisdom is the principal thing. So, as we are searching and seeking for those things that we believe will benefit our lives, by making it fuller, we must consider that without wisdom we will not

have the life we are seeking after at all. Having wisdom as the principal foundation of our lives, we will be able to make wise decisions in seeking everything else we desire.

Furthermore, it is wisdom that recommends us to God, understanding that without Him we are incomplete. Wisdom beautifies the soul, enabling us to answer the end of our creation and that is to return to our creator, living for a good purpose in the world, and going to heaven at the end of our journey.

Gift of Salvation for Non-Believers

"For all have sinned, and come short of the glory of God." (Romans 3:23)

This section was written especially for non-believers, those who have not accepted the gift of salvation. The gift of salvation saves souls from eternal damnation and is a free gift offered by God Himself.

John 3:16-18 says, *"For God so loved the world, that he gave his only begotten Son, that whosoever believeth in him should not perish, but have everlasting life. For God sent not his Son into the world to condemn the world; but that the world through him might be saved. He that believeth on him is not condemned: but he that believeth not is condemned already, because he hath not believed in the name of the only begotten Son of God."*

This section of scripture tells us God's purpose for giving His son Jesus to the world. The world was in a bad condition. The world was overwrought with sin; the people were living for fleshly desires rather than for God's desires.

As a result of the world's conditions, God decided He would offer the perfect sacrifice that would save the world from being a place where people were lost and had no hope. He decided His own son could stand in proxy for the sin-filled world, taking all sin upon Himself.

So Jesus came, born of a virgin, to save this dying world. He walked on this earth for 33 ½ years, doing the work of His Heavenly Father. At the appointed time, He died by way of crucifixion upon a cross at Calvary, on Golgotha's hill. He shed His blood and died for you and for me. Because His blood was pure, it paid the penalty for all unrighteousness and gave those who believe in Him direct access to His father's throne.

Scripture tells us in Matthew 27:51 that the veil of the temple was ripped in two from top to bottom, at the moment that Jesus' spirit left His body. As a result of the veil's removal, we are no longer required to have a high priest make intercession for us. We, as the children of the Most High God, are able to approach the throne of God for ourselves, and Jesus sits on the right hand of the Father making intercession for us.

But what is even more miraculous than God offering His own son as the perfect sacrifice was the fact that when Jesus was placed in grave clothes and placed in a tomb, He only remained there until the third day. God would not have it that His son would remain in the heart of the earth forever. In order for people to believe in the awesome power of God and His dear son Jesus, a miracle had to be performed. So, on the third day, after Jesus died on the cross, He was resurrected, demonstrating the omnipotence of God.

This very act was the act that would cause people to believe in a god that reigns supreme and holds the power of the universe in His very hands, a god that could save them from themselves.

Today, if you are an unbeliever, you can change your destiny. You can change where you will spend your eternity. Our Heavenly Father gives us the freedom of choice about how we want to live our life here on earth and how we want to spend eternity. In Deuteronomy 30:19, God boldly declares, *"I call heaven and earth to record this day against you, that I have set before you life and death, blessing and cursing: therefore choose life, that both thou and thy seed may live."*

So, dear friend what choice will you make today? Will you spend your eternity with the Creator or will you suffer Hell's eternal flames? Again, the choice is yours. Just as the men aboard the ship who were with Jonah became believers, you too can make a choice to accept the only one and true living God as your god.

If after reading the above passages, you have decided that you want to spend your eternity in Heaven with God, the creator, and His son Jesus, and the Holy Spirit, read through what has affectionately come to be known as the Roman's Road. This is the road to salvation. As you read through the scriptures that comprise the Roman's Road, you will also read the explanation for each scripture, so you will have clarity about what you are reading and confessing.

The Roman's Road to Salvation

The road to salvation begins with Romans 3:23 which declares, "*For all have sinned, and come short of the glory of God.*" This scripture explains that everyone has come short of God's glory and needs redemption. Then, Romans 6:23a states, "*For the wages of sin is death.*" Here, we learn that the consequence of living a life of sin is death. Everyone will experience physical death as a result of the sin committed in the garden of Eden, but those who commit themselves to a life of sin will suffer eternal damnation in the lake of fire (Rev. 19). Continue with the rest of verse 6:23 that says, "*but the gift of God is eternal life through Jesus Christ our Lord.*" There is an alternative to suffering eternal damnation. We can accept the gift of salvation by accepting Jesus as our personal Lord and Savior. Then, Romans 5:8 says, "*But God commendeth his love toward us, in that, while we were yet sinners, Christ died for us.*" We are able to receive the gift of salvation because Christ came to earth and shed His blood for us on the cross.

Continue to Romans 10: 9-10 which says, "*That if thou shalt confess with thy mouth the Lord Jesus, and shalt believe in thine heart that God hath raised him from the dead, thou shalt be saved. For with the heart man believeth unto righteousness; and with the mouth confession is made unto salvation.*" If we confess with our mouths that Jesus is the son of God, that He came and died for our sins, and that God raised Him from the dead, we will receive salvation.

Finish with Romans 10:13, which states, *"For whosoever shall call upon the name of the Lord shall be saved."* Call upon the name of God by saying these words, **"Lord Jesus, come into my heart and save me, Lord. I believe that you are the Son of God who came and died on the cross for my sins. I believe that you rose from the grave. I also believe that you now sit in heaven on the right side of the Father, making intercession for me. I accept you as my Lord and my Savior."**

Now that you have confessed with your mouth that Jesus is the son of God and that He died for our sins and rose from the grave, **YOU ARE NOW SAVED!!!!** You will spend your eternity in heaven.

The next step is very important- you must find a Bible-based church that teaches the Word of God and confesses the Lord Jesus Christ to be the son of God. Don't delay. Do this immediately. Do not leave yourself open to the enemy. Get connected with the saints of the Most High God and keep yourself covered with the unspotted blood of the Lamb.

Here is my prayer for you.

Father God,

I thank you for the opportunity to minister your word to the unsaved, the unchurched, and the uncommitted. Father God, I pray now for the souls who have just received the gift of salvation. Lord Father, they have opened their hearts to you, and I know that you have received them into your kingdom and written their names in the Book of Life. Father God, I pray that you will touch their lives and show yourself mightily before them. Let their eyes be opened by the scales falling off, allowing them to see clearly.

Father God, I even pray for the backslider, those who have turned away from you after receiving the gift of salvation. You said in your Word that you desire that none would perish. So Lord, I send your Word to them right now, praying that they would confess the iniquity in their heart, repent, and turn from their evil ways, so that they may receive a life of abundance. You said in your Word in Matthew Chapter 14, that every knee shall bow before you and every tongue will confess that Jesus is Lord.

Father God, I pray now that we all come under subjection to your Word and that we will humbly submit our lives to you. I ask all these things in the name of my Lord and Savior Jesus Christ.
Amen, Amen, Amen!!!!

I will continue to pray for your success in your walk with God. Remember, this spiritual walk that you are about to embark on will not be an easy walk, but remember, the race is not given to the swift but to those who endure to the end.

Be blessed with heaven's best. I love you!

About the Author

Dr. Cassundra White-Elliott resides in California with her family, where as an English/Education professor, she teaches at various community colleges.

When writing, she composes with the direction of the Holy Spirit, in an effort to share with God's people all He has for them.

In addition to teaching and writing, Dr. Elliott also serves as an evangelistic teacher. She is also the founder of International Women's Commission, a ministry that serves the needs of the entire person, by attending to healing the mind, body, soul, and spirit.

Dr. Elliott holds a Ph.D. in Education, a Master's degree in English Composition, and a Bachelor's degree in Education.

Dr. Elliott is the founder and editor-in-chief for *Christian Inspiration* magazine, which covers topics germane to Christian living and the world at large.

Dr. Elliott is also the founder of CLF Publishing, LLC. For your publishing needs, go online to www.clfpublishing.org.

Other Works by the Author

(All books can be purchased at
creativemindsbookstore.com
amazon.com
barnesandnoble.com)

From Despair, through Determination, to Victory!

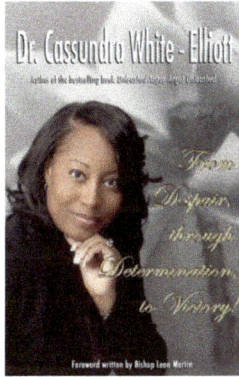

A lot can happen during a span of 40 years. The life of Dr. Cassundra White-Elliott has been anything but uneventful. From a fun-loving childhood sprinkled with incidents of abuse to a tumultuous young adulthood to a stable, secure adult life, she has experienced a full life, with much more to come. Her story is inspiring and motivating.

If anyone lacks hope, reading Dr. White-Elliott's autobiography will propel him/her into an attitude of "Maybe I can." This attitude, if nurtured and developed, will grow into an attitude of "Yes, I can." Throughout her life, Dr. White-Elliott has always held in her heart the belief that she could achieve anything that she had a made-up mind to embark upon. She was determined to achieve her heart's desires, doing what God has called her to do. She takes no credit for herself. All the glory goes to God, for He is her driving force. In Him, she lives, moves, and has her being.

Through the Storm

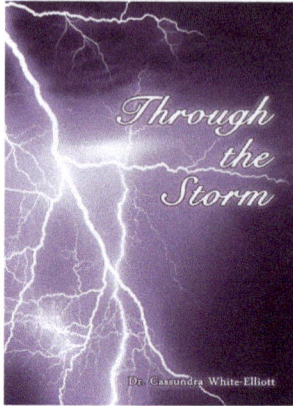

Through the Storm was duly inspired by the avaricious cloud of depression that decided to hover overhead of my daily existence in the latter part of 2007. Although I found it extremely difficult, I was once again compelled to not be defeated by just another snare that the enemy, the trickster, set for me. Once again, or more appropriately I should say *continuously*, he has exerted pernicious efforts to snatch the very life out of me by causing me to wallow in despair and to believe that I had been overcome by failure when in actuality and all reality, I was just experiencing a temporary setback. During those cloudy days, I had to remind myself daily that even though I was a target of the enemy, I am and will always be a child of the Most High God, Jehovah, who is my rock, my stability.

Unleashed Anger, Anger Unleashed

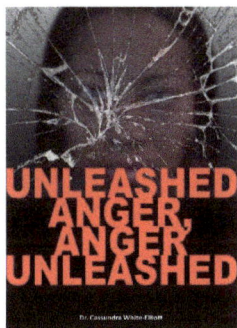

Introduction (snippet)

As I prepared to embark upon the adventure of writing this book, I had to prepare myself to also be transparent. I have found that being transparent is required in order for healing to transpire, healing for all those that peruse the pages of this book and myself. And I may as well tell you that today, at the onset of this project, I have not been totally delivered from my condition of being an anger-filled person. However, I am definitely a work in progress. I have made strides with the assistance of my Lord and Savior, Jesus Christ, who is the head of my life. Without his love, guidance, and teachings, I would not be the woman of God I am today. I shudder to think where I could be instead and will therefore not entertain the thought.

Public Speaking in the Spiritual Arena

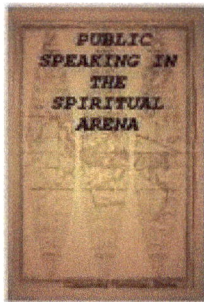

Chapter Two

How Communication Works

Purpose: This chapter will explain the six primary components of communication, identifying their purpose and how they work together.

The Source

In oral communication, the source of information is the speaker. In a church setting, the foundation of the message is God's word, but it is a speaker's interpretation of God's word that is delivered to the audience. As speakers vary, the information may vary but should have a similar essence because the foundational text is the same.

The Message

The message is the collective set of ideas that the speaker (the source) wants to deliver and/or illustrate to the audience. The message can be informative where the speaker informs the audience about a specific set of information. Or, the message may be persuasive in nature if the speaker wants to persuade the audience about conducting themselves in a specific manner, accepting God's commandments, or any number of things.

Where is Your Joppa?

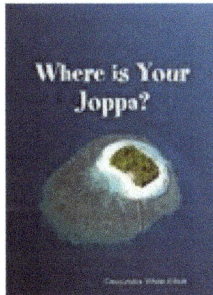

Where is Your Joppa? was written for the express purpose of illustrating God's call for obedience in the lives of believers with respect to the individual call that He has on each of our lives. As you read throughout the various chapters, notice that the emphasis is placed on our persistent disobedience in answering God's call in a specific area of our lives. We have become a people who are similar to the Israelites when they found themselves in the middle of the wilderness, following their exodus from Egypt. Before God, they murmured and complained about their current life conditions and failed to be obedient to God's statutes delivered through His servant Moses. Their persistent disobedience caused them to lose the opportunity to see and enter the Promised Land. I ask you, "What has your disobedience cost you?" "Was your disobedience worth what it cost you?" "Do you think about the souls you could have ushered into the kingdom of God?" These are some of the questions that I pray will be answered through your reading of the book.

Mayhem in the Hamptons

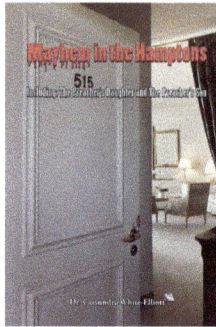

Romero and Yolanda optimistically plan for the day that is going to change their lives from being single persons to a couple who is united in holy matrimony. They, along with their parents, close friends and family, fly over to the infamous Hamptons, where only the rich and famous vacation, to have their dream wedding at the five-star Hampton Suites located on a peninsula in the Hamptons. Little do they know that their perfect day will turn out to be less than perfect when their wedding planner Mariesha Coleman suddenly goes missing!

A time when the newlyweds' lives should be filled with joy and the creation of wonderful memories, they are stricken with grief as they desperately try to find clues to help solve Mariesha's disappearance.

Mayhem in the Hamptons is a tale that shares how the horrors of a woman's past can come back to haunt her in more than one way and the impact it can have on anyone who gets in the way.

Preacher's Daughter

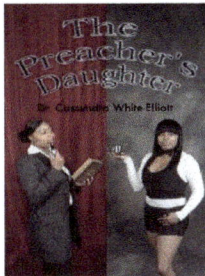

Tinisha, the daughter of a preacher, is a twenty-six-year-old God-fearing young woman endeavoring to complete law school so that she can make her mark in the courtroom. Working in one of the late-night clubs in Hollywood to earn money to pay her own way through school, Tinisha soon learns that life doesn't always go as planned. Finding her strength in her faith, Tinisha constantly finds herself praying as she watches God move miraculously in her life.

Preacher's Son

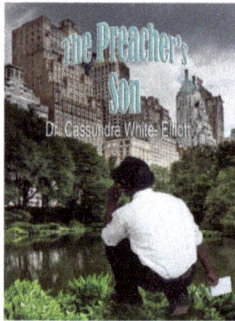

Romero Turner is a private investigator with a promising future. As he continues to build his career, he is excited about the cases he undertakes. However, his father Pastor Theodore Turner has other plans for his son's life. In the midst of trying to save his client's husband from Sylvester Domingo, a ruthless crime lord, Romero must try to salvage his relationship with his father. He must decide if ministry or life as a detective is in his future.

Lord, Teach Me to be a Blessing!

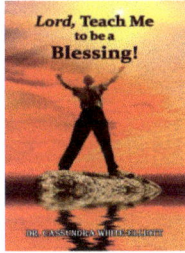

Lord, Teach Me to be a Blessing! will change a person's mentality from being centered around "me, myself, and I" to focusing on "others."

The world system teaches us that it is acceptable to place ourselves above others in an attempt to get ahead and even to survive. Herbert Spencer coined the phrase '*survival of the fittest*' after reading Charles Darwin's theory of evolution. This concept of surpassing and outdoing others is the world's philosophy.

However, the word of God does not subscribe to or promote this self-centered ideology, and therefore, neither should believers. We must hold fast to the truths outlined in Holy Scripture: "*Love thy neighbor as you love thyself*" (James 2:8) and "*It is more blessed to give than to receive*" (Acts 20:35).

While holding God's truths to be self-evident, we must demonstrate them to others, thereby showing them the way of the Lord of how to be a blessing to someone *rather* than looking to receive a blessing.

This is the very purpose of this book: to change the mentality of the world from being *self*-centered to *other* centered.

After the Dust Settles

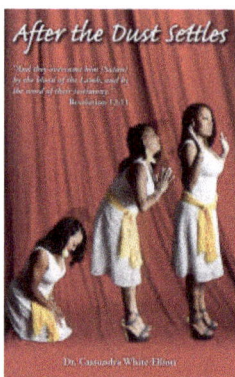

Throughout the journey of life, we all experience ups and downs and joys and pains. Most of us successfully find solutions to the situations/problems we encounter, but we often avoid dealing with the attached emotions. If we continue to ignore the emotions of pain, hurt, disappointment, anger, etc., we set ourselves up for destruction. Our families, our cultures, and our society tell us to be strong, to keep our chin up, and to grin and bear it. However, these methods of avoidance can lead us to strokes due to the undue amount of pressure we place on ourselves and/or mental illness from being unable to cope with the emotional baggage we have accumulated.

In *After the Dust Settles*, Dr. C. White-Elliott shares several situations that we all may encounter at one time or another in our lifetime and how to successfully navigate through them, so we can find ourselves emotionally healthy after the dust has settled and the situation has been rectified.

Begin reading today and experience a better tomorrow!

Claim Your Inheritance

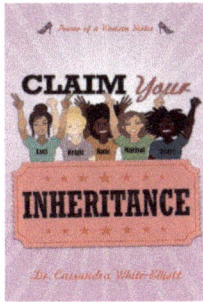

"The thief cometh not, but for to steal, and to kill, and to destroy: I am come that they might have life, and that they might have it more abundantly" (John 10:10).

Satan's mission is to steal, kill, and destroy all that God has provided for us. With him on the rampage, we must be ready to go to war- spiritually and naturally. On the other hand, we could sit idly by and allow the enemy to take what is rightfully ours. However, that is not the will of God. God has given us power to tread upon serpents and scorpions (Luke 10:19) and to reclaim all the enemy has stolen from us.

This book will share how we can be victorious in reclaiming what is rightfully ours when the enemy has turned his ugly head in our direction and made us prey for his latest scheme.

With God on our side, the enemy will not prevail!

A Diamond in the Rough

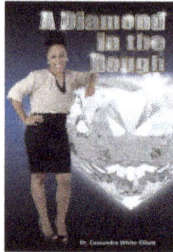

A Diamond in the Rough Architecture Firm was built and is owned and operated by lead architect Kyra Fraser. For the last five years, Kyra has been extremely successful in business, but her love life leaves much to be desired.

Kyra has set high standards for herself and does not wish to take a man in any condition and attempt to make him over. She is looking for someone who is drama free, well educated, very cultured, fun-loving, good looking, self-motivated, and the list goes on.

Will Kyra find the man of her dreams, or will her dream just continue to be a dream?

As you delve into this page-turning novel, Kyra's reality will unfold as you are drawn into her world of design, love and office drama- which includes her best friend's husband who is looking for love in all the wrong places.

365 Days of Encouragement

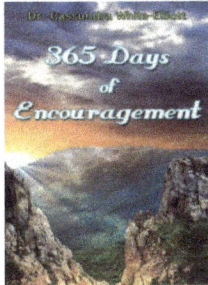

Just as our brain requires oxygen obtained from the air we breathe to sustain our mortal bodies, our spirit requires revitalization and encouragement in order to be strengthened each and every day of our lives. The revitalization and encouragement needed for the spirit of man comes directly from the word of God and assists us in walking according to the way of our heavenly Father. *365 Days of Encouragement* provides a scripture a day for each day of the year. Along with the daily scripture is a brief note of commentary also for the benefit of edifying the saints of God.

It is my prayer that the people of God would live a fulfilled life through Christ Jesus. Knowing His word and understanding we can walk in the fulfillment thereof is empowering. We are instructed in II Timothy 2:15, *"Study to shew thyself approved unto God, a workman that needeth not to be ashamed, rightly dividing the word of truth"* (KJV). Take an opportunity to delve further into the word of God, to know His statutes and to allow your own personal life to be edified, so you can be equipped to bring glory to God and lived a fulfilled life.

A Mother's Heart

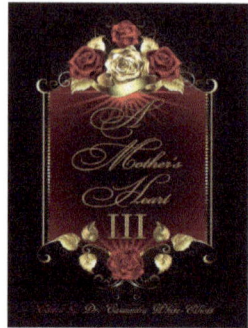

A Mother's Heart shares the unconditional love of mothers through a compilation of testimonies. Each testimony serves as a tribute to a special mother. The children of the represented mothers have lovingly written about their childhood, young adult life and/or older adult experiences they shared with their mother. As you read the writers' reflections, you will feel the expressions of love exude from the pages.

The purpose of this book is two-fold. First, it honors those mothers who stood by their children through the trials of life and showered them with unconditional love. Second, the book is a source of encouragement for mothers who may feel inadequate and question whether or not they are actually suited for motherhood. Our advice to mothers is, "Be encouraged; the journey of motherhood may seem daunting at times and you may shed some tears, but your children will never forget the love you have shown them and instilled in them to share with others."

Mothers may not be perfect, but they are definitely unmatched by any other category of person on God's green earth!

Broken Chains

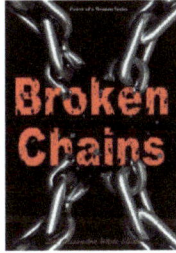

Broken Chains is an in-depth survey of five life-changing tragedies that can and will serve as chains to bind us if we are not watchful and mindful of their potential effects. In our lifetimes, we may all experience death of loved ones, sexual abuse, broken relationships, promiscuity, and sickness and disease. These everyday life occurrences can have detrimental effects on the remaining years of our lives and change our existence, unless we deal with them in a healthy manner.

Broken Chains not only brings to light the detrimental effects of five life-changing tragedies, but it also shares how anyone who experiences them can be healed and delivered from their effects.

If you have experienced death of a loved one, sexual abuse, a broken relationship, the effects of promiscuity, and/or sickness and disease and have not been able to rid yourself of the emotions attached to them or specific resulting behaviors, Broken Chains is for you.

God designed each of us for a purpose, and He has an intended end for us to achieve. In order for us to effectively achieve our God-given purpose, we must be free of chains that bind us. It is not God's desire that we become immobilized by life's events. His desire is for us to be healed, delivered and set free. Be healed today, in the name of the Lord Jesus Christ!

I Have Fallen

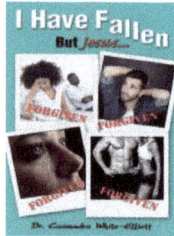

Do you know anyone who has committed his/her life to Christ but has done something unseemly that you would never expect a Christian to do? How did you feel about that person or what the person did? Did you pass judgment? What if that person were you? How would you feel if you made a misstep and no one forgave you and instead began to treat you differently? How do you feel when you are judged for past mistakes or lifestyles that are no longer part of your life?

This book shares four true stories of Christians who have made missteps during their walk with God. The purpose is not to air their dirty laundry, but to demonstrate our humanness and our vulnerability. None of us are exempt from making errors and falling into sin. It can happen to any of us.

The solution for these dilemmas is for the person who fell into sin to make a life-changing move and turn away from the sin, repent and ask God for forgiveness. His arms are waiting!

The next solution is for those who witness the sin or know of it. Pray and be of comfort to the one who has fallen. Lead him/her back to the path of righteousness. Love thy neighbor and treat him/her as you want to be treated!

The Bottom Line

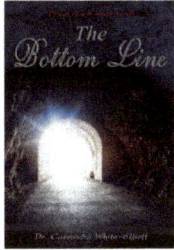

The Bottom Line is a detailed review of the Book of Job. Much can be said about Job's experiences with the loss of his children and wealth and the subsequent return of it all in mass proportions. However, the telling of Job's story in the Holy writ was not intended to focus on the return of his wealth. Instead, the focal point should be on the bottom line of the entire situation.

When you experience trials or tragedies in your life, do you tend to focus on the trial itself, the result, or the bottom line?

"What is the bottom line?" you may ask. The bottom line is the message God is sending regarding the situation.

When Job experienced his tragedies, there was a bottom line. Likewise, when you experience your trials and tragedies, there is a bottom line as well. It is up to you to discover it.

This book will reveal the bottom line in the Book of Job. It is readily apparent, but many often overlook it.

Now, it is up to you to uncover the bottom line of your experiences, for God will not bring a trial to you without a good reason.

Power of a Woman

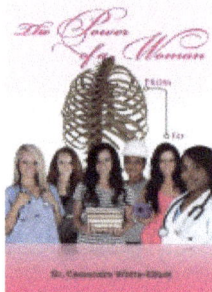

The ongoing conversation about the value of a woman is presented from a different perspective in *The Power of a Woman*. Dr. Cassundra White-Elliott presents a biblical perspective of women and compares it to the worldview of both yesterday and today. This comparison seeks to illustrate God's intended purpose for His uniquely designed creation: woman. Dr. Elliott shares God's truth about pre-imposed limitations set by man versus the limitations God Himself set for woman in addition to the wealth of liberality He gave her.

Women's creativity and abilities are not meant to be stifled. They are meant to be utilized to bring glory to God, to help sustain and nurture their families, and to move the world forward. Knowing God's truth will show women how to celebrate and appreciate who they are as well as one another!

Women, let's take the blinders off, lift our heads up, and march forward, side by side with men, and bring glory and honor to God! Take your rightful place with a gentle smile and grace and be who God called you to be!

Power of a Woman Series

Time is Running Out!

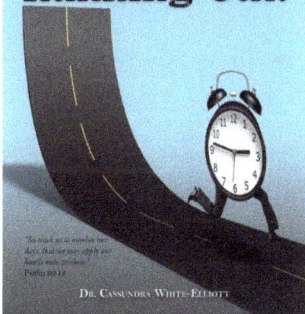

So teach us to number our days, that we may apply our hearts unto wisdom. Psalms 90:14

Dr. Cassundra White-Elliott

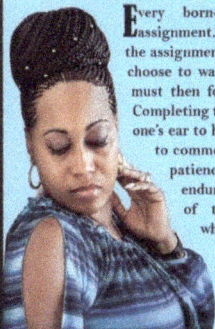

Every born-again believer has a God-given assignment. Whether or not the individual accepts the assignment is a personal decision. For those who choose to walk in God's will rather than their own must then follow God's divine plan for their life. Completing the God-given assignment means tuning one's ear to hear, receiving guidance, knowing when to commence, and, most importantly, exercising patience. Furthermore, the task may require enduring hardship along the way. A servant of the Lord can never fully anticipate what may occur during the journey of completing an assignment. What should be foremost in the individual's mind is completing the task, so he/she can hear the Master say, "Well done."

If you have never completed a God-given assignment, or if you are preparing to embark upon a new journey designed by the Lord, this book is for you. It will provide guidance for commencing and completing God-given tasks. If you feel intimidated by the task ahead, don't be dismayed. The Lord said He will never leave you or forsake you (Hebrews 13:5). Trust and believe that He will be with you every step of the way.

But you must act now!
Time is running out!

CLF Publishing, LLC.
www.clfpublishing.org

Dr. Cassundra White-Elliott's books are available at:
www.creativemindsbookstore.com
www.amazon.com
www.barnesandnoble.com

ISBN 978-1-945102-21-9
90000
9 781945 102219

Set Free

If you possess habits and display characteristics that are unbecoming, debilitating, and hinder the desired progress in your life or that affect your relationships with others, Set Free will provide the steps you need to be healed and delivered, through the Word of God.

Deliverance is available to you! Claim your healing today and walk in victory!

Do You Know God?

Have you or someone you know ever felt alone, confused, or unsure about your walk with God or are you unsure of what being a Christian is all about? ***Do You Know God?*** is an excellent text for providing answers to many of your questions. This book introduces adolescents and young adults to God in addition to answer many of their questions about being a Christian. This book shares the testimonies of the trials and tribulations that other teens have experienced and how God prevailed in their lives. All the information that is shared on the pages of the book is based upon the Word of God and the scriptures are taken from the King James Version of the Bible. If you are interested in knowing more about God's Word or how to begin your Christian experience, this book is for you.

Daughter, God Loves You!

"...for her price is far above rubies"
(Proverbs 31:10b)

Dr. Cassundra White-Elliott

Maybe you have heard the proclamation, "The world is going to hell in a hand basket!" Well, I believe I must concur.

However, I do *not* believe, we– the adult, mature believers- should sit idly by and allow our daughters (and our sons for that matter) to go with it! We must fight for our girls and young women, for they are the mothers of tomorrow, and some may even be young mothers today. Not only will they continue the human race, but also they can have bright futures in their careers and as leaders in our society, as they allow God to direct their paths and order their steps.

Daughter, God Loves You! is an earnest attempt to address many of the issues that plague our society and turn our daughters' heads away from God.

In this book, we dive head first into topics such as God's love, the importance and impact of education, the effects of social media, overcoming abuse, and the proper perspective of the future.

For the young adult women- Reading this book will empower you to have a bright prosperous future from being enlightened about the dangers that plague our society and how to avoid pitfalls, as you walk along the path God has paved for you.

I invite all of you to take this journey with me to save our daughters and yourselves (young women) from corruption, by being empowered with knowledge.

We must thwart the plan of the enemy. So, LET'S GO!

CLF Publishing, LLC.
www.clfpublishing.org

Dr. C. White-Elliott's books are available at:
www.creativemindsbookstore.com
www.amazon.com
www.barnesandnoble.com

ISBN 978-0-9961971-9-9
90000

9 780996 197199

Web of Lies

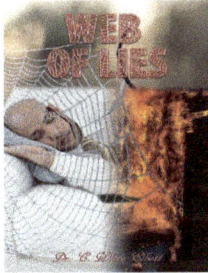

A year ago, Charlito Jimenez was found in his den, lying on the couch, with a fatal gunshot wound in his temple. Everyone in the community still wants to know who is guilty of the unfathomable crime.

Tinisha Salisbury, attorney at law, has taken the case of the accused. Can she prove her client's innocence or will a guilty verdict be rendered?

Halfway through the trial, a badly burned body was found at the scene of a fire.

Is there a string of murders being committed?

Are the murders related?

Web of Lies spins the tales of several characters into one web. Each has a story to tell, and everyone has something to hide. The web of lies, deceit, and revenge take over the lives of these characters to the point where they may not be able to see their way clear.

Embracing Womanhood

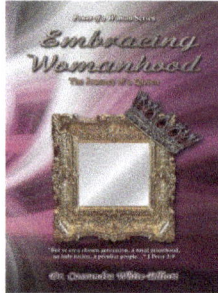

The journey from adolescence through puberty to young adulthood can be challenging and quite disconcerting for the average young lady. The changes that occur both mentally and physically can be both confusing and uncomfortable. However, the outcome of the changes can be beautiful. What she will experience during this time in her life is simply a metamorphosis – taking off the old and embracing the new. The process is similar to that of an awkward caterpillar that overtime develops into a beautiful, graceful butterfly.

The topics covered in this book (puberty, self-esteem, mental stability, goals, finances, and relationships) will assist young women (ages 15–23) in understanding the transformation they are enduring to prepare them for the life that lies ahead. After taking in the information, they will literally witness themselves evolve from princess to queen!

The Making of Dr. C.:
A Memoir

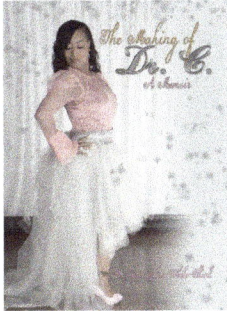

The Making of Dr. C. shares the 50-year journey of Dr. Cassundra White-Elliott. Her journey of trials, missteps, successes, and triumphs will inspire you to face any trial you may encounter with a positive attitude and the Word of God.

Her life demonstrates no matter what you may face, there is always a brighter tomorrow.

Keeping the faith will allow God to work in your life. After all, He only wants the best for you!

Prepare for Battle

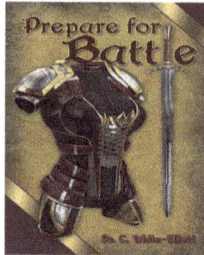

The very life you live is a war zone, riddled with battles ranging from the unexpected to the inconceivable to the paralyzing. The only way for you to successfully navigate through each battle unscathed or with minimal damage or loss is to equip yourself with the full armor of God, which consists of the girdle of truth, the breastplate of righteousness, the gospel of peace, the shield of faith, the helmet of salvation, and the sword of the spirit. To seal your victory, prayer is just as essential a component as each piece of armor. Therefore, the seven aforementioned items serve to comprise the arsenal necessary for winning wars.

This book goes to great lengths to explain each piece of armor in depth, with use of commentaries. The more you understand the importance of the arsenal, its function in battle, and how to effectively use it, the better prepared you will be when unexpected or inconceivable or paralyzing battles confront you.

Equipping yourself today for battle, with the full armor of God, will prevent Satan, our adversary, from annihilating you.

Safety in Him

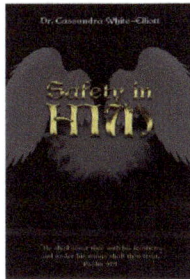

Luke 21:33 declares, *"Heaven and earth shall pass away: but my words shall not pass away,"* and Jeremiah 1:12 says, *"Then said the Lord unto me, Thou hast well seen: for I will hasten my word to perform it."* According to these two verses, we can stand firmly on the Word of God at all times because His Word is everlasting, and He watches over it continuously to perform it.

While the promises of man may go unfulfilled, God's Word is true and He declares, *"So shall my word be that goeth forth out of my mouth: it shall not return unto me void, but it shall accomplish that which I please, and it shall prosper in the thing whereto I sent it"* (Isaiah 55:11).

In this book, particular attention is brought to Psalm 91:1-7. In these verses, God promises His divine protection for His children. Read Christopher's story and see how the divine protective nature of God is demonstrated and remember Acts 10:34b, which states, *"God is no respecter of persons."* What He is able to do for one, He is able to do for another. So, no matter what you be faced with today, call on the Lord, and He will deliver you!

Women's Study Bible

NEW INTERNATIONAL VERSION

Red Letter Bible

CLF PUBLISHING, LLC

Learn the Bible Series

(26 books from A-Z to teach children biblical
principles and prominent characters.)
Currently available are A-Q. More coming soon!

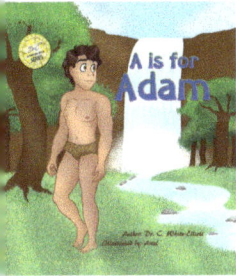

A is for Adam

B is for Babel

C is for Christ

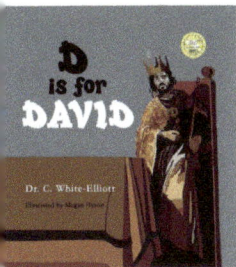

D is for DAVID

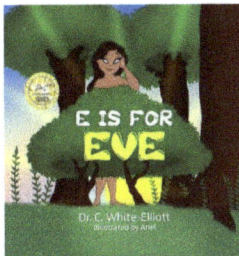

E IS FOR EVE

F IS FOR FORGIVENESS

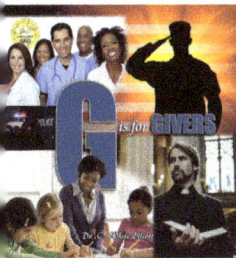

G is for GIVERS

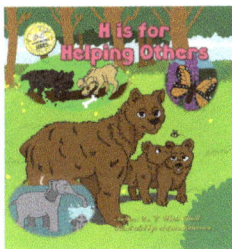

H is for Helping Others

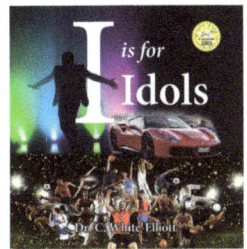

I is for Idols

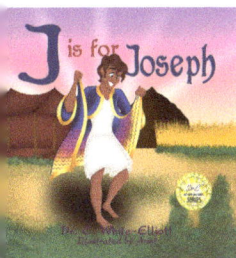

J is for Joseph

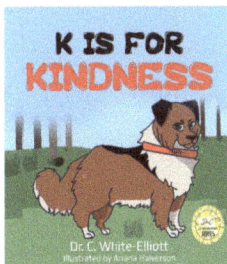

K IS FOR KINDNESS

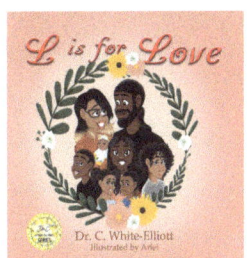

L is for Love

Christian Inspiration is a quarterly magazine with issues released each year in January, April, July, and October. The magazine covers topics germane to Christian living and the world at large.

DR. CASSUNDRA WHITE-ELLIOTT

THE LAST SHALL BE FIRST

AN ANALYSIS OF THE SYSTEMIC SUBDIVIDE OF BLACK AMERICA

Beginning in the early 1500s, Africans were transported to America; however, they were not permitted to live and operate as free citizens in the new land. They were enslaved and treated as property rather than human beings. Some 500 years later, people of African descent and other Blacks have yet to realize the true meaning of freedom, equality, and liberty in America. This inequity stems from sustained and systemic racism and acts of discrimination. These abhorrent acts have consistently kept Black Americans marginalized from mainstream America, depriving them of equal access to employment, education, wealth, housing, quality health care, and safety.

The modern-day slavery experience of Africans in the 1500s and 1600s (which led to the current condition of Black Americans) was similar to that of the Israelites of the 15th century B.C. as they too were enslaved. At the moment of the Israelites' liberation from Egypt, God moved mightily in their lives by transferring the wealth (gold and silver) of Egypt to the Israelites.

In this season, God desires to move mightily in the lives of Black Americans as He did for the Israelites. And, just as He did for them, He wants to complete the wealth transfer that has already been initiated, for the Bible says in Proverbs 13:22b, "...and the wealth of the sinner is laid up for the just."

So, what must you do to prepare for a mighty move of God? How can you be an agent of change?

CLF Publishing, LLC.
www.clfpublishing.org

Dr. Cassundra White-Elliott's books are available at:
www.creativemindsbookstore.com
www.amazon.com
www.barnesandnoble.com

ISBN 978-1-945102-62-2
90000
9 781945 102622

Rest in HIM

Scriptures for Daily Peace

Dr. C. White-Elliott

Each day brings about its own unique challenges. Yet, in the midst of the challenge you are enduring, there are scriptures that are applicable to your situation that will provide insight, understanding, and comfort. God's Word serves as our guide and provides peace in the midst of a trial or daily circumstance. The Word of God keeps us healthy and whole when we read it, meditate on it, and apply it.

Rest in Him provides Bible verses at your fingertips for easy use. Keep this handy tool close by, so you can remind yourself that the Lord is an ever-present help in the time of need.

CLF Publishing, LLC.
www.clfpublishing.org

ISBN 978-1-945102-68-4

90000

9 781945 102684